"If There's Anything I Can Do ..."

Carlene Vester Eneroth

Published by
Classic Publishing
P.O. Box 9208
Spokane, WA 99209

Contact Classic Publishing
for information on quantity discounts.

ISBN 1-879331-01-2

DEDICATION

To the forever memory of my "then" husband, Greg Vester and to my wonderful "now" husband, Don, who first taught me to laugh and to love again, then encouraged me to start our "Solitaires" support group and finally, never gave up his hope that I'd write a book...this is the result.

ACKNOWLEDGEMENTS

My special thanks to my group of "Solitaires*" (just like a diamond Solitaire, even though we stand alone, we can shine brilliantly and be attractive.)who have shared willingly with me of their walk (and falls) along the survival road; also to other acquaintances who became friends as they shared their experiences in times of deep grief.

Most important, thanks to my Heavenly Father, without Whose peace, love, comfort and shelter, I would never have made it back from the edge of the grave.

* Group name suggested by Mary Brite, *Triumph Over Tears*. Nashville: Thomas Nelson Publishers, 1979.

PREFACE

Many of the illustrations that are shared here are from my own support group of "Solitaires." As each of us has lost a mate, we find ourselves uniquely bonded together in our monthly meetings. Many of the day-to-day circumstances, roller-coaster emotions and outside pressures expressed, are common to all. At the top of our "Wish We Could Change List" is the description of us by the world as widows. Although it accurately describes who we are, the sound of that word and all the mental images that go with it, makes us shudder. So, in this book, you will not find that word. It has been replaced with survivor. That is what we are.

The idea first grew from reading the following poem by Beverly Romey:

SURVIVOR

I learned I was a survivor.
It was in the paper.
His obituary read,
He is survived by his wife, Beverly, of the home.
I didn't want to survive.
I wanted to die too.
Death had to be easier than surviving!

Surviving! I learned to survive.
I survived the sleepless nights,
Tortured days, endless weeks,
Holidays, Sundays,
Months of hopelessness.

Survival of the fittest.
I became strong.
Amazingly now, I'm proud
To be a survivor.
I deserve a medal for the battle scars.*

*THEOS magazine, "Grief Steps I: Voices of Experience",
Pittsburgh, PA. Used by permission.

TABLE OF CONTENTS

INTRODUCTION

"If there's anything I can do . . ." How many times have you sincerely said that to friends, relatives, neighbors or members of your church who have

suffered a loss or are experiencing a deep, personal tragedy? Our natural tendency is to reach out to help in some way but we are at a loss to know what would be most appreciated during this time.

That was certainly my experience until I was put on the answering side of that statement. My husband, Greg, was 31 when he suffered a fatal heart attack after water skiing. Suddenly, I was in that complete fog that envelopes the grieving person's mind, actions and whole being. At this same time, people were telling me, *"If there's anything I can do . . ."* Only then did I begin to realize that just attempting to logically answer that leading statement required clarity of thought of which I was incapable at the time.

The easy way out was to simply reply, "Nothing right now." Later, as the days, weeks and months dragged slowly by, many little things came to mind that I wished friends would do, but by then, they had assumed I didn't need any assistance and that I was probably "over it." How wrong that assumption was!

Do you know someone who is hurting right now, wandering around in that emotional fog, devastated by some loss? Someone who is struggling to endure one twenty-four hour period at a time? You must be vitally interested in their survival because you're looking through this book. Great! Its purpose is to provide specific, practical ways to help so you won't ever have to say, *"If there's anything I can do . . ."* You'll already be doing it, unasked.

CHAPTER ONE
THE FIRST DAYS BLUR

Whether you've heard the news by mail, phone call or visit, you now know that someone has died and a family has been left behind. You obviously want to help. Read this chapter through and pick out specific suggestions that you feel comfortable doing. As you strive to be thoughtful and caring, be assured that you are that and that your actions are appreciated, although your deeds of love may not be acknowledged for some time.

Food

Many people want to assist the bereaved person by bringing food to the home. That is a good idea, as cooking for themselves and the family is at the bottom of the Have-To-Do scale for awhile. But friends assume that labeling their dishes is the easiest way to have the empty plates returned. However, when Greg died, as I was overwhelmed with loads and loads of main dishes, salads and desserts, I saw my neat, orderly kitchen turned into a Goodwill counter of stacked and cleaned dishes and plates. Who was going to see to their return? Me! Because a person's mind is completely overcome by all the details of just plain living, even this small task seems impossible. It would be easier to leave off your dish, saying you'll return on a particular day and pick it up. If your church takes a dinner to the home, assign someone to tell the family who will be by, on what day, to pick up the containers.

As a special friend, neighbor or relative, you might take on the task of keeping a written record of what food was brought by whom. Again, it is difficult for a survivor to think of these details and their attention is stretched in many directions. Yet they want to be able to write thank-you's and acknowledge people's thoughtfulness. A small notebook or pad and pen by the front door would help keep this list current. Leave room to check off each name when a thank-you has been written.

Continue to think of dropping off food at the survivor's home in the weeks to come. A survivor finds cooking has no appeal whatsoever right now. Why should they cook when there's no one to cook for? Why even bother buying groceries? No one is home to care and besides, the survivor has to pass shelf after shelf in the store that is loaded with items their loved one used to enjoy so much. When you are making a pie, a meat loaf or Jello salad, double the recipe and then call the survivor. Don't give an option about them wanting the food but just say, "I've made two pies (or salads, etc.) today. Do you want me to bring one over for you this afternoon or tomorrow morning?" It is especially nice to see someone at the door in the next several weeks with something for you. What a special way to say, "I know you still hurt and I was thinking of you."

Household Needs

When death comes suddenly, many household tasks need quick attention but the surviving person's mind cannot focus on them clearly. Drop by the house and take the laundry home. There is always some to be done and beds that need to be stripped and remade with fresh sheets for arriving family members.

Drive by the home and offer to mow the lawn or trim the shrubs. People are so relieved to have their homes presentable both inside and out. If the death occurs during the winter, stop and see if they need the sidewalks shoveled or the driveway cleared so there's room for visitors to park their cars.

Flowers

It is certainly heartwarming to see flowers at the church or funeral home and to know people were thinking about the survivor and their loss. However, because sending flowers is a love expression commonplace to so many, you might try a different approach. Save your floral delivery until a week or two has passed. The funeral bouquets have wilted by then, the constant flow of visitors has subsided, the house is quiet and the full realization of the loss is just beginning to surface. Then the florist arrives, handing the survivor a feminine arrangement that speaks of life and of loving friends. Terrific!

Did you know that your opportunity to pen a note on the floral card is also noticed? I'd always assumed that just signing my name would be sufficient...those receiving them would hardly notice anything else. Not true! Some of our friends in California were unable to attend the funeral. Their love and care for me was abundantly evident with the delivery of a lovely bouquet some time after Greg's death. Written on the card was their paraphrase of Psalm 56:8: *"He bottles our every tear; He remembers our every sigh."* I have never forgotten that. You might write, "I care that you hurt." "When no one else knows how this feels, He does." "We miss him too." "I care that it hurts just to breathe."

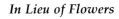

In Lieu of Flowers

Would you like to put your money toward something more necessary than flowers? Here are some alternatives:

1. Take a package of thank-you notes and some stamps to the house. It was obvious that I was going to have multitudes of those to write. But after using what the funeral home gave me, I didn't feel like wandering through the stores to find more notes, let alone standing in the Post Office line for stamps. (Why is it we rarely seem to have on hand just what we most need?) Nothing was more practical for me than to receive a sheet of stamps and some thank-you cards. Now, I remember how special that was for me and do the same for other families. The response is always the same: gratitude, surprise, appreciation. The credit is not mine...it is just recalling someone else's kindness to me.

2. Many survivors are waking up to feel that chest-tightening fear of "What do I do for money right now?" "Can I get money from our checking account?" This fear is very real. Immediate financial obligations may include clothes for the funeral,

a plane ticket for a college student, or even gas in the car. Instead of flowers you might include that money in your sympathy card.

3. Send a Memorial Gift Subscription. For the loss of a spouse there is the THEOS* organization. The initials stand for "They Help Each Other Spiritually" and their ministry is to reach out to survivors. For eighteen dollars they will send an eight-issue magazine series, written for hurting families. Each issue includes a cross-section of first-person stories and feature articles, addressing the concerns of the recently bereaved. At six-week intervals, an issue is mailed to survivors, providing continuing support over an extended time period. The eight issues are:

1. Grief Steps I: Voices of Experience
2. Grief Steps II: Mutual Help and Hope
3. Grief Sounds I: The Grief Process
4. Grief Sounds II: Through Grief to Renewal
5. Days & Seasons of Grief: Holidays, Anniversaries
6. Grief, A Family Affair: Mutual Help Within Families
7. Grief & Sympathy: What Grievers Want From Friends
8. Singles, Pairs, Social Circles: Socializing, Remarriage

*The address for THEOS is : THEOS, 1301 Clark Building, 717 Liberty Avenue, Pittsburgh, PA 15222

In the death of a child, parent, sibling, friend, loss in miscarriage, etc., a subscription sent to a new survivor from **Bereavement Magazine*** is a wonderful idea. Each issue addresses a variety of topics and areas of concern, nearly all of which are written by those who are journeying that survival road. The editor herself is a survivor of the death of her teenage daughter and so that first-hand knowledge of grief is always evident in the magazine's format and articles chosen for print. The cost for one year is twenty-two dollars but another option is to give a gift of four issues for twelve dollars. The magazine's goal for each subscription is worth mentioning here: 'Thanks for the opportunity to be in touch. We'll keep visiting until you don't need us any more ... And, from the heart we can say, 'We'll share your satisfaction the day you decide **not** to renew your subscription.'

Wow! What hope that gives a new survivor: this **will get better!**"

Cynthia** expressed the imiportance of these magazines in this way:

"The first issues were my literal lifeline for awhile. I would anxiously get home from work and check the mailbox to see if another one had come. If it had, then

*Bereavement Publishing, 350 Gradle Drive, Carmel, IN 46032
**To provide privacy, the names of survivors have been changed.

I would spend the rest of the evening reading through each comment, on each page, empathizing with each article. I could not have received a more useful and necessary gift."

Sympathy Cards

There are a wide variety of cards out on the store shelves today, aren't there? People spend a lot of time trying to pick out just the right one. But there never seems to be such a thing as a "right one." The act of sending the card is far more impressionable on the survivor than a "right" verse. In fact, I read very few of the printed verses on cards I received because the sentiments expressed were far too real for me to handle emotionally. Instead, I would often skip down to the signature. And there is where the difference was . . . between the common sympathy card and the one that was written just for me. Cards that were and still are precious to me were the ones that penned something about my husband. People would remember something funny we had all done together, maybe a part of his personality they had observed, some occasion when he had helped them or some characteristic of his that stood out to them. Those cards naturally brought on the tears but also smiles of pride and gratitude too. I only wished he could have been there with me to read what people thought of him!

When you're signing your name, stop for a minute and add some specific recollection.

Survivors With Young Children

These families have problems totally separate from the older survivor's point of view and sometimes can use the help of interested friends on a more urgent level.

The parent of the children may not feel it appropriate or necessary for the children to attend the funeral. Why not offer to babysit them for her and thus relieve her mind? Children still want to talk about what is happening to them so give them this freedom when they are with you. It is amazing to see how deeply even very young ones are affected by a death in the family and it is important that they not be stifled in their curiosity and questioning.

In the weeks and months to come, continue to keep the young family members in mind. If you're taking your children to the park or the zoo or for an outing in the country, invite these children to come along. Many times their parent desperately needs to get away . . . from the memories stored in the home . . . from the same routine that gives them too much time to think . . . to just be able to give vent, perhaps, to the emotions they are keeping locked inside so as not to frighten the young ones. What a relief to have someone volunteer to keep the children occupied for a few hours! The survivor can get away for a long walk or a drive or even just do some window shopping.

If the father has died in the home, the boys are especially feeling the loss of a male influence. Try to get the boy enrolled in your city or church's Big Brother Program. If there is no group like that available, encourage a group of men in your church to take on the young family as a project. When the thought is presented that we, as a church, can minister to this boy just by invitation and thinking ahead, many are willing to help. The church men could see to it the boy is invited to club meetings with ones his age, or check to see if fees are paid for him to attend summer camp. Maybe he wants to play in Little League but doesn't know where to sign up or doesn't have a way to earn money to participate. Call and ask if he or she wants to go out and hit some balls or play catch or work on pitching techniques. A parent doesn't usually have the time or inclination right now to get this involved and would be so appreciative of this kind of support. Take an interest, give suggestions and be available just to listen and show that you care. It will make such a difference!

Roxanne was one of the first members of our "Solitaire" group. Widowed in her twenties, she had three young children. The daughter couldn't discuss her father or even bear to have his name mentioned around the house. A year went by and finally her mother called me and wondered if I knew about any books available for children on the subject of a parent's death. Fortunately, I found a wonderful book compiled by Jill Krementz entitled, *How it Feels When a Parent Dies*. It is written from the children's viewpoint, ages five to eighteen, as told to the author. It covers a variety of causes of death including terminal illnesses, accidents, heart attack, and suicide. I left this book off with Roxanne. Her daughter sat down and read it through from cover to cover. When she finished she kept saying, "Be sure to thank Carlene for that book." If it's available at your library, leave it off with a survivor in the coming weeks. It gives new insight to both the children and their grieving parent.

Someone I Love Died, by Christine Tangvald is a new book in print, written for children. The "fill-in-the-blank" format is unique and gives the child the opportunity to fill in the name of the person that is missed and also write a line or two about how they feel right now. At the back of the book is

something special I think **all** survivors would like
to have: A pull-out poster. Space is given for the
child and any adult who might want to help, to
relive and write down special moments of being
with the sister/brother, parent, grandparent, who
is gone. Some categories include "His favorite color
was:" -- "Favorite thing we did together:" -- "I
remember something funny." What a treasured
time it is to fill out and put up this poster which
provides visual proof that there **was** such a person
on this earth and although they are now gone, they
certainly are **not** forgotten!

IN CHURCH

First Greetings

It was amazing to discover how difficult it was to return to my church. For many, this is one the tougher times. Why? One of the main reasons is that well-meaning friends crowd around to express their concern and sorrow. They have the best of intentions but it doesn't take long for the survivor to become dissolved in the very tears they have been trying so hard to hold in check while out in public. Linda agreed:

"I had the hardest time in church that first Sunday morning . . . I didn't think I could even keep breathing. Everyone crowded around, trying to tell me they were sorry until I thought, when I started crying, I would never stop."

Send your cards or flowers or take in your food but when you meet the survivor on Sunday, just smile and mention you're praying for them but do not linger.

Music

Hymns and music touch the grieving heart as nothing else. It is soothing and comforting in one's own home where there isn't the worry about losing your composure. There, you can play the records over and over and cry along with the words and yet be unobserved. But it's a different story when you are part of the church congregation.

I had always enjoyed music in church and played cassettes in the car and records at home. But until Greg died, I did not realize how much my heart and ears were connected to my tear ducts! It seemed as though every hymn in church ended with a verse about heaven. Here I was, alone in a pew, instead of sitting as I normally would, with my husband, trying to sing about his new home. For weeks, those last verses would leave my hymnbook tear stained. Eileen shared:

"When you talked about this effect of hymns on a survivor a year ago, I thought the whole idea seemed kind of silly; what could be so hard about singing some hymns? But then Larry died and all of a sudden, I was dissolved in tears. Music and hymn wordings do make a difference!"

What suggestions can be given? Obviously, it is not too practical to abolish singing for a period of time in the congregation, following a death! But the sensitive song leader can choose to sing only three of the four verses, leaving out the last one if it closes on the theme of heaven.

Those in charge of special music segments of the Sunday services might be careful in their selections as well. Dovie found this to be true when she returned to church after Charlie's funeral. Dovie explained:

> "That first Sunday became even more un-bearable because of the special music. The solo-ist dedicated her singing of "Be Still My Soul" to me. Words like...
>
> 'Be still my soul: thy God doth undertake,
> To guide the future as He has the past;
> Thy hope, thy confidence, let nothing shake,
> All now mysterious shall be bright at last...'
>
> just finished me off! I felt like a brick wall was collapsing on my lungs, making it impossible to get my breath. I know she meant well but I nearly suffocated!"

Donna had a different, but equally traumatic experience. The second anniversary of her husband's death was on a Sunday. The church thoughtfully met her at the door that day with a floral bouquet. But as she settled into her place at the organ, the song leader announced, "Because this is the anniversary of Ray's death, we're going to honor his memory by singing the same songs selected for his funeral." And there sat Donna, totally unprepared for this, trying to play the organ and keep her memories and emotions in check.

Singles

Avoid suggesting that the newly bereaved person take part in your Single's Group. In your opinion they may have suddenly changed marital status to the "single" category but this is not how they view it. In talking with survivors from twenty-one to eighty-one, they all agree: "I am not single. I was married . . . I thought in that way . . . lived that way .. . related to that lifestyle. I cannot go back to what once was, no matter what other people think. I will always be married in my own eyes and it's almost blasphemous to suggest that I suddenly fit into a single's group like some teenager again."

Perhaps you will notice a survivor's interest in attending your group. By all means, then, invite them in and make them feel welcome. But let the initial move come from them.

CHAPTER THREE
WHAT WILL I SAY AND DO?

Most people enjoy visiting and talking with friends—until those friends are in the grieving process. Then the visit or invitation extended becomes an obligation and goes to the bottom of their priority list. All kinds of thoughts naturally run through their minds . . ."What should I say?" "What if I say the wrong thing?" "If they cry, it will be all my fault." If you feel that way, like so many others, the guidelines listed here are just for you!

Stopping For A Visit

It is best to remember that your visit in itself is evidence of your concern and thoughtfulness. The survivor does not expect you to have the answers to all their questions. They only ask that you be there to listen as they reminisce about the past, share the present and contemplate a future all alone. By keeping this in mind, the visitor can feel greater confidence and more at ease as they go to listen and to talk.

There are three DON'TS:

1. *Don't* tell the survivor "time will make it better." This is a favorite phrase everyone repeats

and although it is absolutely true, don't bring it up. Why? Here you are sitting with someone who is struggling to get through the hours of today and trying to face tomorrow. She desperately wishes someone could make these minutes, days and weeks pass quickly, but nothing can be done about it. Clara said:

> *"I kept hearing time would make it ok so I wished with all my heart that I could crawl in a hole and hibernate for a year and when I crawled out again, everything would be OK."*

Although a great idea, that is not an option! They have to endure one hard day at a time. Someone phoned me right after Greg died and casually said, "I hear it takes two years to get over something like this." I wanted to shout at the receiver: "Thanks SO much! Here I am trying to live through the rest of today and you tell me that in another 730 awful, endless ones, I'm going to begin to feel better??" I could have done without that kind of advice!

2. **Don't** say, "I know how you feel." You simply cannot know. No one can fully understand what the grieving person is experiencing because every circumstance, marriage, family situation and time frame is completely different. People might say, "I lost a brother (or sister or mother) and so I know just how you feel." A survivor wants to look them in the eye and almost laugh outloud as they mutter

to themselves, "You certainly do NOT!" All losses are heartbreaking. Of particular agony is the loss of anyone living in the survivors home. The minute-by-minute reminders in each room of that home speak of the person who is gone and are incredibly difficult to handle.

It is important to remember that the death of a parent, especially to a young child or teenager living at home, is truly traumatic and forever life-changing.

Nate was sixteen when his dad died suddenly in December. He shares:

"I'm now happily married and have a great life. When my wife wonders out loud what she can do to make Christmas a more exciting holiday for me, I have to tell her, 'Oh, it's ok the way it is.' It's just that Christmas has never been the same since my Dad died."

Try saying, *"I don't know how you feel but I care that it hurts."* That immediately lets the survivor know they are experiencing something which you cannot understand and that it is not to be lightly dismissed.

3. **Don't** promise to come by and visit or have the survivor to dinner or go shopping together sometime and then not follow through with your idea. It is easy to blurt out these things at the funeral or in church the next week or when meeting them on

the street..."I'll have to stop by and we can sit down
and visit." "We'll have you over for a big roast beef
dinner real soon." "Let's get together for lunch
sometime." This may appear to be an innocent
remark on your part and soon after you've said it,
it's forgotten. But to someone who is alone and has
nothing to look forward to, it's not forgotten! The
thought of someone coming by or inviting them
out, gives a glimmer of hope to the days ahead.
After a few months, though, the survivor realizes
you are not going to follow up your suggestion and
there is a letdown. Each of us survivors can specifically recall just such instances. We do not hold it
against that person but it serves as a constant
reminder to us not to give out empty promises
to others.

So . . . there you are, talking to a grieving friend
and all of a sudden you hear yourself saying one
of those phrases. What to do? When you arrive
home, get out your calendar and write a notation
of the survivor's name at the bottom of that month.
This will visually remind you to keep current on
your promises—if not that week or the next, at least
during the coming month.

Well, you say, if I leave out your three DON'TS,
what is left for me to say or do?

DO listen. The survivor finds great comfort for
a few months, in getting to repeat the story of the

death of their mate. They may break into tears and the telling of the story might make you uncomfortable, but they find release in being able to tell it again and again. Sometimes the repeating of this traumatic time makes the death a more certain reality to the survivor. Cry with them, if you feel like it. Don't admonish them not to cry. The survivor's system needs to find release in tears. As you listen, do not feel you are bringing on tears that were not already going to fall. The survivor will most likely be using the tissue box frequently whether you are listening and talking with them or not.

DO ask questions. What is getting easier for the survivor now? What is getting harder? How are they sleeping? Eating? What is it like going back to work, or finding a job perhaps or handling the children alone? Sometimes I think people appear to be earning points toward a special award being handed out to those "Most Able To Work Their Way Around A Single Subject Without Bringing It Up!" They would visit me at home or talk with me at work and mention politics, gardening, the weather, schools, sports-anything BUT what was happening to me. For me, this loss was the biggest thing in my life; it was about all I could focus on. I felt such utter frustration when friends wanted to discuss everything but what I was living through right then!

DO brag on them. Visitors need to realize that the person who would normally be home with the survivor, listening to all the details of their everyday life and problems, would also be there to brag on that person . . . about a good meal, their efforts to keep the checkbook current, handling the children or noticing a new dress or hair style. Now that positive feedback is missing and this leaves a huge gap in the survivor's ability to look at themselves with any confidence. Brag on what they have been accomplishing alone. They have been sleeping alone; gone back to work. They are paying the bills now, attempting to keep up the house, taking care of the children, writing thank-you's, cleaning out closets and drawers with their mate's belongings. They are unable to chart their own progress. Most likely they feel they are losing ground instead of moving ahead. They feel unorganized, scatter-brained and useless. To have someone from the outside specifically point out areas of advancement brings a real boost!

DO mention the name of the one who has died. Until Greg died, I thought the most considerate visitor was one who never brought up the name of the deceased, never mentioned incidents in which the person had been involved and who glossed over the whole event. I was wrong! Now, how I longed to have people say, "When we were at the dinner buffet, I thought of Greg. Wouldn't he have had fun getting his money's worth?" Or "I was remembering how he liked to kid you. He was a riot when he was doing that!" These comments may bring on the tears again, but they are coupled with a warmth that lets them know their mate is not forgotten. Otherwise, they feel as though the loved one is never thought of or remembered by anyone other then themselves.

Dale and Gina lost their son in his early twenties and found this same situation. They would try to bring up his name when talking to their relatives. But an instant freeze would come over the dinner table as someone would quickly think of a way to change the subject. The parents reflected:

"Why won't they let us talk about him? Do they think we have forgotten and they do not want to remind us? We are never going to forget! We wish they could realize how much better we feel when we get to talk about him and what we are thinking and feeling."

DO ask men how they are. Maybe you find yourself in another habit I thought most appropriate: when a couple had lost a child or had a miscarriage or stillbirth or a parent or relative had died, I would always ask the *husband* how the *wife* was doing. By trial and error, I discovered: Men have feelings to be considered too! One fellow questioned, "Why do people always ask *me* how my *wife* is doing? Don't they think I experience any grief in all of this? Don't I count? Why can't they just ask how *I* am?"

Another man gave me insight into the expectations we have for men in times of grief:

> *"The business world is especially regimented in terms of grief. They willingly give you three days off work for a death and then expect you to be back to work and just fine after that. They don't anticipate you having any more problems with grief and simply believe you should be handling your workload just fine. They fail to realize your grieving hasn't even begun and yet they expect you to be over it in three days."*

Sundays

Sundays are hard days—not just in church, but because it is such a long, long day, with very little to keep a survivor busy. Most people have that day off work. Many shopping areas are closed and TV is minimal in both choice and appeal. The day drags on and on. I used to be the first one to volunteer on Sundays to work — anything to not have to stay home alone. Of course, one can attend church but even *that* seems lonely because everyone appears to have a partner. When the survivor leaves, it is easy to assume that most everyone else in church is going home to a family dinner or going out to eat and yet they go home to an empty house. Be especially thoughtful on Sundays. Is your family going out to dinner? Invite a survivor to go along. Are you going to check out some garage sales you missed on Saturday? Or going for a drive in the country after church? Tell a survivor when you will pick her up to go along. The day is made more bearable by being around other people and attending events with somebody.

Dinner Invitations

 Thoughtful friends will continue to think about a survivor eating alone and invite them over for a meal or out for lunch during the noon hours, if they are working. Breakfast get-togethers are an inexpensive but a very nice way to start the day.

Maybe you've issued several invitations only to be turned down? Don't give up! It takes some time and a special courage to decide on accepting an invitation. The survivor wonders if they will feel like a fifth wheel. Will returning to a friend's home alone bring back too many old memories? Sometimes, too, survivors are just getting used to the deafening quiet that descends on an "alone" home at night and they cannot bear the thought of going out, enjoying themselves and then having to return home and readjust to the quiet again. Older survivors may be fearful of getting out at night. They feel quite vulnerable alone. Offer to pick them up and bring them home after dinner. Walk them to the door and be sure they are in safely, with the lights on. This type of thoughtfulness is most appreciated.

CHAPTER FOUR
GRIEVING . . . HOW LONG?

That is the ultimate question! It is important to understand that every fiber of one's being is shaken to the core by death. Common practices and daily habits become impossible chores. Whether it is sleeping, cooking, eating, writing letters or even making phone calls . . . every thought and action literally requires a physical struggle. Many people experience health problems as they grieve: stomach ailments, headaches, hair falling out, fingernails splitting. Some even discover their jaws sore only because they are daily clenching that jaw to keep their emotions under control.

One thing is certain . . . it is not "over" just because you see the survivor laugh sometimes, finally go on a trip or two, clean out the child's room and turn it into a study or guest room, get a new job, hairstyle, car or even go on a date. **In fact, the loss has accurately been described as something you never get over, you just get used to.** If this truth could be grasped and believed by friends, they would not expect the grieving person to spring back and be their old selves again — carefree, going on with life like nothing has happened.

That Third Month

The third month following the funeral is sometimes the hardest. Why? No survivor is sure. It is partly because the dense fog they have been living in since being asked, "Where do you want the body to go?" has been lifted. They begin to mentally function a little more and in so doing, realize anew how much their mate is missed. Slowly, they recall little events or private jokes and times of fun they will not be having again with that person. They continue to find visual reminders… his sweatshirt at the back of the closet, a sock in the bottom of a drawer, an old birthday card, favorite record or see that achingly familiar signature on an old check. Each discovery brings a new wave of emotion. Since everyone is trying to tell the survivor that "time heals," they assume all others *except* themselves are getting better with each passing day. That is not so! In describing this time, Kathi said:

> *"Those days were so horrible! I existed in a state of shock — my whole life — my whole future — even my past — was on BIG BLUR! Would I ever see the sunshine in my life again? The slightest bit of tension between family members and I would have to run and get away from*

it! My mind and heart were totally scrambled. Nothing made sense. Nothing mattered anymore."

The teenage son of Ted and Esther had drowned in a canoe accident. Some weeks after the memorial service, Ted related their feelings:

"What now? Somehow we must go on. We drag ourselves through the days and dread the nights. Physically we are exhausted and mentally we are drained. No one can relate to such a tragedy unless he or she experiences it."

In those first weeks and months of deep despair, you as a friend, are a most vital tool to aid in the recovery process. Try to send a note or card, even flowers, to acknowledge this hard time, especially the third month date. This lets the survivor know the worst month may be passed, although you must not assume that they will instantly get better. The hard days will start to spread out with a *few* slightly better days coming into view. It is encouraging, however, just to hear someone mention how hard things *still* are and at the same time, hold out a light at the end of what seems to be an endless tunnel of hopelessness.

Concentration

Did you know that a survivor's concentration and mental processes are profoundly affected by grief? That was new to me! I thought of myself as young and mentally alert; an organized person, whose favorite hobby was reading. Suddenly, with Greg gone, I could not read through even one page of a magazine. My concentration had disappeared. I would hear what people said to me and then instantly forget it. Someone would explain a job to me at work and the next day, have to repeat the same instructions. Verna empathized, "My mind is still pretty foggy — I can't remember some place I have gone by all my life or the name of someone I've known for years!" What a relief it is for *all* of us to finally know that all of this is *normal*. The human brain is only able to handle certain amounts of stress along with everyday decisions. With the death of a mate or a child being at the top of the stress list, it is obvious the brain is overloaded and loss of concentration is nature's way of using short-circuiting to prevent breakdowns. When a survivor or her friends do not realize this, they naturally assume the person is going crazy. Midge exclaimed, "I'm so *glad* you told me that! I thought I was getting Alzheimer's disease because I couldn't remember or concentrate on anything!"

For some survivors, the lack of concentration may last for many, many months. For others, the time frame of stress-induced memory loss is much shorter but no less shocking. Eleanor shared:

> *"A year after Lyle's death, I found old Christ-*
> *mas cards I'd received that first December.*
> *Going through them, I began rereading com-*
> *ments of friends and found that I remembered*
> *reading none of them the previous year. My*
> *mind was a complete blank on what they had*
> *written!"*

Try not to be impatient with a person living through this perplexing period. The concentration and memory will slowly return and improve. Knowing its cause makes acceptance a little easier.

Gray Days

Sometimes, for no apparent reason, a survivor wakes up to find the whole world is gray. Oh, it may be sunny and warm on the outside, but for the hurting individual, everything inside appears dark and cold. Much of the bafflement experienced by survivors lies in the fact that these days cannot be predicted. Frequently, they come, *not* on anniversaries, birthdays or holidays, but just pop up on an ordinary day — with no warning. Ellie described hers:

> *"I just wake up and suddenly, the whole*
> *world is awful. I try getting dressed, going for*

a walk or a drive or baking up a storm in the kitchen . . . anything! I wish I knew what caused them."

Vicki added:

"Now, after a few months, I am starting to get the feeling that this 'wintertime' around my heart will pass and in its place will come the peace and beauty of spring. But I still have the times when for absolutely no reason I am completely overcome with my loss. It comes as somewhat of a surprise to me because we were told right from the start that Gene had a maximum of ten years and we were lucky to stretch it to thirteen."

Vicki expresses an interesting point! Often observers of the grieving (and even survivors themselves) assume that if they have been living with the fact of a terminal illness for some time, they should 'be prepared' and be able to handle this grief process much better than those who received no advance warning. But I have found this not to be the case. In fact, in talking with many gals who fit this category, it seems they have even a rougher time for awhile.

At first, I was puzzled about this myself but then realized that they are not only grieving over the loss of a spouse but over the loss of an established *lifestyle.* For many, their lives have been put on hold as they have trudged through the maze of doctors, specialists, chemotherapy or kidney dialysis. Their family life has come to a halt in terms of 'normal' functions, conversations, trips and even budgets. And now, with the loss of this intense focus they've had, a double measure of distress is felt. So don't expect more from a 'forewarned' survivor. Remember, they are just as surprised as you might be, at their inability to 'bounce right back!'

Regardless of where the survivor is in terms of their grieving, it helps when you let them know that the intrusion of these 'gray days' is common; they will happen to everyone enduring a loss. And because you understand this, it will be easier for you to follow through on some of the many suggestions listed in these chapters to help the survivor come through these surprise times.

Holidays

 There is no harder time for a new survivor than the holidays that approach throughout the year. We all think of Thanksgiving and Christmas as major events that could be the roughest, but it is good to keep in mind that some families have had special family traditions around Easter or even the Fourth of July and so these dates, too, are difficult.

Mother's Day and Father's Day loom as impossible days to get through following the death of a spouse or a child. It is very touching when friends acknowledge this difficulty by making a phone call, sending a card or note or even planning to do something with the survivor on these days.

Often, a special family dinner is part of the yearly tradition. Volunteer to have the dinner at your home, if that is not customary. Having unfamiliar surroundings in another family member's home does not bring back quite so many haunting memories of holidays gone by.

Do help with the dinner. You could arrive early and help mash potatoes, make the gravy or even entertain the children while dinner is being prepared. There is something hard about being in the kitchen fixing food and knowing that someone special is not going to be there enjoying it. Anita said:

> *"I fixed Thanksgiving dinner and didn't have to worry about salting the turkey or the potatoes — both were well-salted by my tears while I was preparing them. Fixing the meal was the hardest part of the day."*

Gloria agreed and added:

> *"The hardest part of any holiday dinner for me is fixing the turkey. It reminds me Ed is not here to eat and enjoy the day and it is so hard*

to hold back the tears. After it is in the oven,
then I'm ok."

Suggest a change in the menu if the survivor is in agreement. When turkey is the usual fare, a prime rib roast or a ham dinner substitute might make fixing and serving the dinner much easier.

Valentines's Day is a vulnerable time. The survivor imagines every other person in the universe is getting flowers, cards, gifts and most important of all: being told they are loved. This would be a wonderful occasion to send a small bouquet or pick out a special card to send, letting them know you realize this day represents another tough hurdle.

Christmas looms as the most dreaded of days, in part because preparation for its celebration begins cropping up in the stores during October and does not end until the New Year. One cannot even go grocery shopping during this time, it seems, without hearing Christmas songs and carols piped in throughout the store. The closer December gets the more merry everyone else seems to be and the survivor agrees with Doris who exclaimed, "Christmas? Bah-humbug!"

Be available to go Christmas shopping with the survivor. Suggest going to a new mall or section of town where she might not usually have shopped. Go early, when the stores open, because it is not as crowded with merry shoppers. Ask if you can help

her wrap presents, mail off packages or even address Christmas cards. Doing these jobs alone is
almost asking too much of the human spirit.

Suggest the survivor (if financially able) treat
herself to a special present. She could wrap it up
and then open it Christmas Day. The privilege of
buying gifts for a mate cannot be replaced, but this
activity gives her an opportunity to get something
she really wants, just to spoil herself!

My mother gets credit for coming up with the
best Christmas idea: A big Cheer Box. Because I
was unable to be with my family for Christmas,
when Mom visited in November, she brought with
her a big box, filled with all sizes of brightly-
wrapped gifts. She recommended I open one at a
time each day through December. She had bought
me knee-highs, a cute pot holder, travel kleenex, a
dishrag (you can always use a new one!), station-
ary, stamps, fancy napkins, etc. None of these gifts
were of priceless value but their worth to me cannot
fully be expressed. When I was having a bad day
at work or some special Christmas music had done
me in for that time, I knew when I got home, there
would be another present to see. If I woke up to
those "gray day blues," I knew I could go find
another package and smile for a minute. Not only
did it brighten every day for that month, but it also
eased me into the holiday spirit. I do not think

anything else could quite have accomplished that. I have, since that memorable first Christmas, given Cheer Boxes to other survivors and suggested it to some church groups and families and each time it has been a big hit!

It must be remembered, that none of the ideas shared here will make the "first" holidays wonderful, no matter how hard you work to help someone. There will still be tears and aching hearts. These suggestions only serve to remind those who are grieving that friends are not so caught up in the holiday spirit as to be unaware of their situation. Your efforts to help will not be in vain and never will be forgotten.

Why Not Get Away?

Be cautious in dispensing this advice as a cure-all for the grieving person. Some believe a survivor should immediately get out of the house . . . go on a cruise . . . take a warm-weather vacation. . . visit a favorite spot from the past. When you are the friend, looking in at the grief cycle, you want the survivor to "get over it" as quickly as possible. To you, the idea of a vacation . . . a chance to get away from work or the house and kids seems ideal. But the survivor finds she cannot "get away" from it all.

They, too, desperately wish to find themselves
anywhere but at home — some place where the sun
will shine again and that black cloud overhead will
disappear. However, they quickly learn that geog-
raphy does not change what is happening in their
lives. The problems do not leave because of a
change in location. So, as a friend, do not have
unrealistic expectations for the survivor as they
leave on a trip. Mary remembered her first trip very
well:

> *"I went to my sister's home in Utah with a
> feeling of great relief; I was out of the house and
> away from responsibilities hanging over me,
> yet amazed to discover I couldn't run away
> from the hurt. It stayed with me. Any travel-
> ing just was not the same without Tom. I could
> hardly believe it."*

Mary added that her advice to another survivor
would be to travel where relatives live because it
helps to have that sympathetic person to cry along
with them.

Traveling alone is usually a new experience and
there is an unsettling vulnerability felt in it. Many
a survivor mentions that having her wedding rings
on gave her a small sense of security. She was not
just sitting on a crowded plane or waiting out a long
airport layover...feeling available to anyone!

When the trip is completed, even though it has

been a good break, the survivor has to return home. Usually this brings another unwelcome surprise for she finds no one there to share in the review of the trip. Only the walls are listening to her plane adventures, lost luggage woes or of the sights she has seen. She may even feel guilty because she did not have the kind of fantastic time everyone expected of her and thus believes she let down her concerned friends.

Knowing this, be quick to visit a survivor just back from vacation. Be sensitive to her desire to share. Brag on her for traveling alone and reassure her it is quite normal to have found the first vacation somewhat less than perfect.

Moving

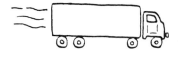

A new survivor has to cope with thoughts of location change that seem to bombard the mind: Should she live in a condominium? Is her house too big now that she is all alone? Does it hold too many memories? What about moving to another town? Should she be closer to her children? Many are urged to make quick decisions on these major issues but that is not always wise. It would be good for friends and relatives to remember that no pat solution in this area works for each individual. Each person's situation is different: each has a different family makeup, changing finances and outside considerations as well.

It is suggested by others that a person wait a year before making any major decision, especially concerning a move. That is a good guideline to follow, but again, circumstances (especially lack of finances) may necessitate a change sooner.

Remain supportive in ideas expressed but keep in mind the fact that the survivor will be changing her opinion many times in the first weeks after a death. Connie, a close friend of two new survivors, observed:

> *"As I listen to Nancy, I am really surprised to see that she is saying many of the same things that Irene did after Charlie's sudden death. Both of them change their minds on where to move or if to move and what to do, so many different times . . . within days or even hours of the last decision. But I have learned now to expect that so I just listen and let them talk."*

As survivors are inundated with so much advice from so many, they are sometimes unable to sort it all out, let alone respond logically to it. As Connie learned, "listen and let them talk."

AS TIME GOES BY

The company has returned home, the food brought in has been eaten or frozen, the thank-you's have been written, the mail load has slowed and the business details are gradually being worked out. Only now is it apparent to the survivor that "normalcy" as she knew it, is not going to return. This is the time for sensitive friends to put into practice other ideas given here.   Underline a few suggestions you feel comfortable doing and then . . . go for it!

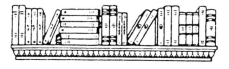

Books

There are a variety of books out on the market today dealing with grief and coping with a loss. Some survivors instantly gravitate to them, spending a lot of their time finding out what is happening to them now and what they can expect in the days to come. Others, however, find that with their concentration level so low, attempting to wade through a book brings only frustration.

In the many books given to me, I somehow felt

an unspoken pressure that if I would just read this-or-that particular book, it would solve most of my problems and answer my endless questions. It did not seem to work out that way for me, and it took me many months to be able to absorb and appreciate what was in some of them.

Books I found helpful later included:

Triumph Over Tears by Mary Brite, Nashville, Thomas Nelson Publishers: 1979.

Without A Man In The House by Wilma Burton, Good News Publishers, Westchester, 1978.

By Death Or Divorce, It Hurts To Lose by Amy Ross Young, Denver, Accent Books, 1976.

By far, the most helpful book I saw is by Doug Manning entitled *Don't Take Away My Grief*. It covered so many of the questions left unanswered by other paperbacks and I rate it at the top of the Survivor's Best Seller Guide.

So, do you pick out a book and take it to a survivor or do you wait? When you have visited them recently, have you noticed some unread paperbacks stacked on their coffee table? If so, ask questions. Is it hard to concentrate on the books when you try to read? Do they not say much to help you? Is it too much work just to read? This will give you an idea of their needs. Explain that you have read a list of books that are recommended by other survivors and you would be delighted to get them a copy of one if they wish. The decision can then be left up to them.

When you decide to take a book, refrain from asking, later on, how they liked that particular selection. Wait for them to tell you. They many have only been able to read through the introduction or cover just one or two chapters. Your asking for a reading update will cause them unnecessary guilt at not being appreciative of your choice.

Calendars

As a firm believer in a calendar, I highly recommend the practice of keeping one current to friends who want to help survivors. Here are some important uses:

1. It gives monthly reminders to have the survivor over to dinner or to go visit them.

2. You can list the deceased one's birthday, the couple's anniversary date and the date of their death and then acknowledge those dates.

3. You can note the third month anniversary and even a six month one and be planning ahead to invite them to dinner or take them to lunch.

Where can you locate these dates? The birth date is usually listed in the obituary notice, as well as the date of death. Your church office may have the couple's anniversary date or you can ask for it from one of their relatives.

When those dates are coming up on your calendar, look for cards to send that say, "I am thinking of you." Even a funny card that makes them smile for a moment at the mailbox is always appreciated. Make reference on the card to this particular day and then that you are thinking and praying for them. Often, it is sufficient to know someone *still* remembers and cares. The tendency of most people is to assume, "If *I* ignore the birthday or anniversary and don't send a card, I won't be reminding them of it." But remember: Survivors are not *ever* going to forget those dates so you might as well acknowledge them yourself. Years will not diminish the memories of those birthdays or the precise moment they experienced "til death do us part."

Recently, I found out that survivors appreciate cards on the death date even though many years have passed. Tom and Eileen lost their son nine years ago. I had only casually known them at the time and not until Greg's death, did I think too much about their loss. Several years passed and then I discovered one day, an article about their son and found the date of his death listed. Noting it on my calendar, I sent some flowers and a card to them at that time. Their reaction amazed me: both of them called and Eileen also wrote to express their thanks. They said that month is still always hard for them, even after all this time. Having someone still remember their son was special. They added:

> *"We don't need the sympathy ourselves*
> *but what is important to us is that others are*
> *still keeping him alive in memory. It is a tribute*
> *to him for us to get a card."*

That expresses it so well and served to remind me again: acknowledge those tough days even when years have gone by.

Men Can Help Too!

It is easy for men to assume that sending cards or flowers and even stopping by to visit are a woman's responsibilities. Often that is true. But there are specific jobs only a man can adequately handle.

For example, when your wife invites the survivor to dinner, check out her car to see what it might need. Does the oil need changing? Does she know how to check it herself? How is the tire pressure? Windshield washer fluid on empty? Suggest a competent mechanic or place of business for her car tune-up. Offer to put on her snow tires or to take them off.

When you are driving in her neighborhood, have some tools with you. Stop and see what tasks could use your touch. Does the outside water need to be turned off for winter? Is a faucet leaking? A light bulb on a high ceiling burned out? Does the weather stripping need replacing at the back door? Is there a dead doorbell? Does she need help trimming the shrubs or planting a garden or fertilizing the lawn?

All survivors at one time or another need help in these areas but are hesitant to call for it. By calling, one feels like they are showing the world they are not handling this "alone" business too well and that they are revealing their mechanical ignorance. There are many little nuisances during each day that makes them feel this way. So when someone offers to give assistance and will even teach them how to run the air conditioner, or change the furnace filter, or fix the sprinkler head, they are a quick study and your unsolicited efforts teach them to be more self-reliant. That is a good feeling but hard to come by!

My husband and I heated our home exclusively with wood. However, he died before getting in our winter supply. Can you imagine my delight, relief and gratitude when I came home one day and found a huge wood supply split and stacked for me by the men of our church?

Cemetery Visits

Survivors react to the cemetery in their own way, at their

own pace. Friends and relatives need to exercise patience and understanding even when a survivor's actions seem somewhat strange.

Some find great solace in just being at the cemetery; comfortable as they "talk" with the one who is gone, useful in leaving flowers as a reassurance their relative is not forgotten or just to meditate.

Others, however, find no special peace at the cemetery and go only on Memorial Day while some never go at all. Often, the most trying cemetery visit seems to be the first time a griever goes to see the headstone now in place or view the writing on the crypt.

Ask if the survivor would like company on this visit. I was surprised to discover how difficult it was to see Greg's name and date of his death down in black and white. I was viewing this many months after his death and yet the stark finality of it really hit me like a bolt out of the blue. I'm glad I didn't have to go alone that first time.

You may be taken by surprise that you, as a good friend, also feels a strong emotional pull while there at the cemetery. Share how you feel with the survivor. It is good to know others are feeling this loss afresh as they are with you.

CHAPTER SIX
ARE YOU PREPARED?

No one is ever totally prepared for a tragedy to come their way. No one marries with the thought of losing that special mate or rejoices in the birth of a child and yet pictures planning their funeral. But God permits death to touch our lives in many ways: through our friends, relatives, neighbors, in our church or in our immediate family. There are guidelines listed here by which you can better prepare your family for this time that will come.

1. Get a safety deposit box or a strong box in your home and then be consistent about keeping all your important papers in it. This would include your Social Security number, veteran's papers, insurance policies, will, etc. If you live in a state that has Community Property laws, ask your attorney about the advantages of signing a community property agreement and a Power of Attorney agreement. It could save you a tremendous amount of time and pain avoiding probate.

For those who are left, it is so easy to go straight to one location and know you will find all the information you need there, instead of running around the house, going through drawers and boxes in the closet, attempting to collect the information various companies and banks require.

2. Talk about death, what you want for a funeral service and how you wish to be buried. I know this seems to be a forbidden subject to cover, but I only hope that in reading through the pages thus far, you have seen what death can do to the mind and will then realize that any knowledge you can give, preceding a death, makes all details later so much easier to handle.

I was the spouse who never wanted to pay for insurance, did not want to hear details about death or have Greg always mention, "Now that is one song I want sung at my funeral." But when I went from the ski boat to the emergency room and they said Greg was gone, it was a wonderful relief to watch the Lord give me instant recall. I clearly remembered Greg's wish to be cremated and then just have a memorial service. I even knew what music he would want to have. The survivor wants to plan a funeral the way the deceased would want it, but if they have never discussed the situation, the planning will be done with a gnawing thought that "maybe he did not want it this way."

Try to plan a few specific but short periods of time to discuss these things. Obviously, the topic is not anyone's favorite! Make it easier on each other by talking about a few of these things and then having a date for dinner. Spending an entire long evening on this one topic could leave each mate more than slightly depressed.

3. Tell your spouse what you want done with your things, your tools, your jewelry. I do not think there is one survivor who does not wish they could recall their mate from heaven for even just thirty minutes, to receive advice on what they wanted done with this-or-that. To have been told ahead of time would be such a comfort.

4. Be a teacher in the home. Show your mate how to pay the bills, which ones are due when (such as property taxes), what ones are automatically deducted from your bank account and how to write a check. Paying the bills together as a team gives understanding in the confusing world of finance to both partners.

Ladies need to be teachers as well. Does your husband know how to operate the stove and microwave? How to fix a few simple meals for himself? Can he master the dials on the washer and dryer? Sure, someone can always show him when you are gone, but when it is already so difficult to concentrate and remember instructions, why not make it easier by letting him already be familiar with the appliances.

5. Organize your tax records for each year. Keep them in the same place where they are easily accessible. One of our Solitaires was audited by the Internal Revenue Service a few month's after her husband's death. Because she could not quickly lay her hands on the tax information they requested from a filing two years previous, she was forced to pay the penalties.

6. Discuss future plans and goals. Mora said, "I wish I could have talked with Tim about the goals he had for the children; what he wished for them in the future."

Others have added, "I wonder what he thought we would do in retirement . . . would he want me to sell the house?" "Should I move to a condo?" "Should I live in the same town with my children or move away from them?" It is difficult to talk about a future in which you will have no part, but for the sake of the one who is left, DO IT!

7. Be wise in what you say about remarriage. When a survivor is ready to date again or think of remarriage, the one thing they want most, is to be able to know they have the approval of the one who is gone. Some gals have to live with the fact that their spouse told them not to remarry or perhaps even extracted this promise from them while on their deathbed. When they attempt to make this new kind of life for themselves, they will be overwhelmed with guilt for going against your expressed wishes.

You may think, "Oh, I am only *kidding* when I tell her I will come back to haunt you if some other

guy ends up spending my insurance money!"
Maybe you are kidding but she will remember
what you said and take it very seriously if contem-
plating remarriage.

Occasionally friends and relatives may not
understand someone remarrying. They cannot see
how one can "replace" that special mate; it cannot
be done. The Lord has made each person different
and no one is an exact duplicate of another.
However, people may question in their minds how
the survivor could have two husbands. The Lord
graciously gave me this example: parents who
have more than one child, love each one yet each
one is different. They did not stop with just one
child because they would not have the capacity to
love a second one. They made room in their hearts
for a unique, special, additional offspring. And so
it is with survivors beginning a second marriage.

Finally, having your household in order takes
thought and timely preparation. When Greg died,
one of the special cards I received was from a friend
of my parents. It read in part:

"I hear you and Greg planned for so many
special vacations. But isn't wonderful that he also
prepared for his last, must unexpected trip?"

This is certainly true in the spiritual sense and
because of that, I know Greg is now enjoying the
delights of Heaven. But it is also true in the business

sense. He had learned as a teenager following the death of his father. Observing the excellent provisions made for his mother, Greg wanted to be sure he did the same for me . . . that we had a will, community property signed, some insurance and even discussed funeral ideas. He was prepared for his last, most unexpected trip! I trust that this, too, could be *your* family's description of *you,* were death to suddenly come.

CHAPTER SEVEN
IT IS UP TO YOU!

Congratulations! You have finished the last chapter and worked your way through the whole book . . . because you cared enough to learn and to be prepared. There will always be new survivors out in the world — of all ages, stumbling ahead of sliding back on the survival road. They long to have someone nearby who will know how to help when they encounter those gray days, contemplate that first cemetery visit or have a special family holiday approaching. And now they have that someone . . . in you!

Keep this book available as a quick reference guide. Review the suggestions from time to time. Share it with others who may have said, *"If there's anything I can do . ."* but never have received a reply. For you see, the vital ingredient that makes this book work is **people like you** — who care enough to invest their time with someone who hurts and then, in turn, make others aware of some easy, practical ways to show their interest and concern as well.